Volume 2

God Speaks,
Are You Listening?

A Twelve Week Discipleship Bible Study

Christine Cloninger

Becoming Whole in Christ
Ministries

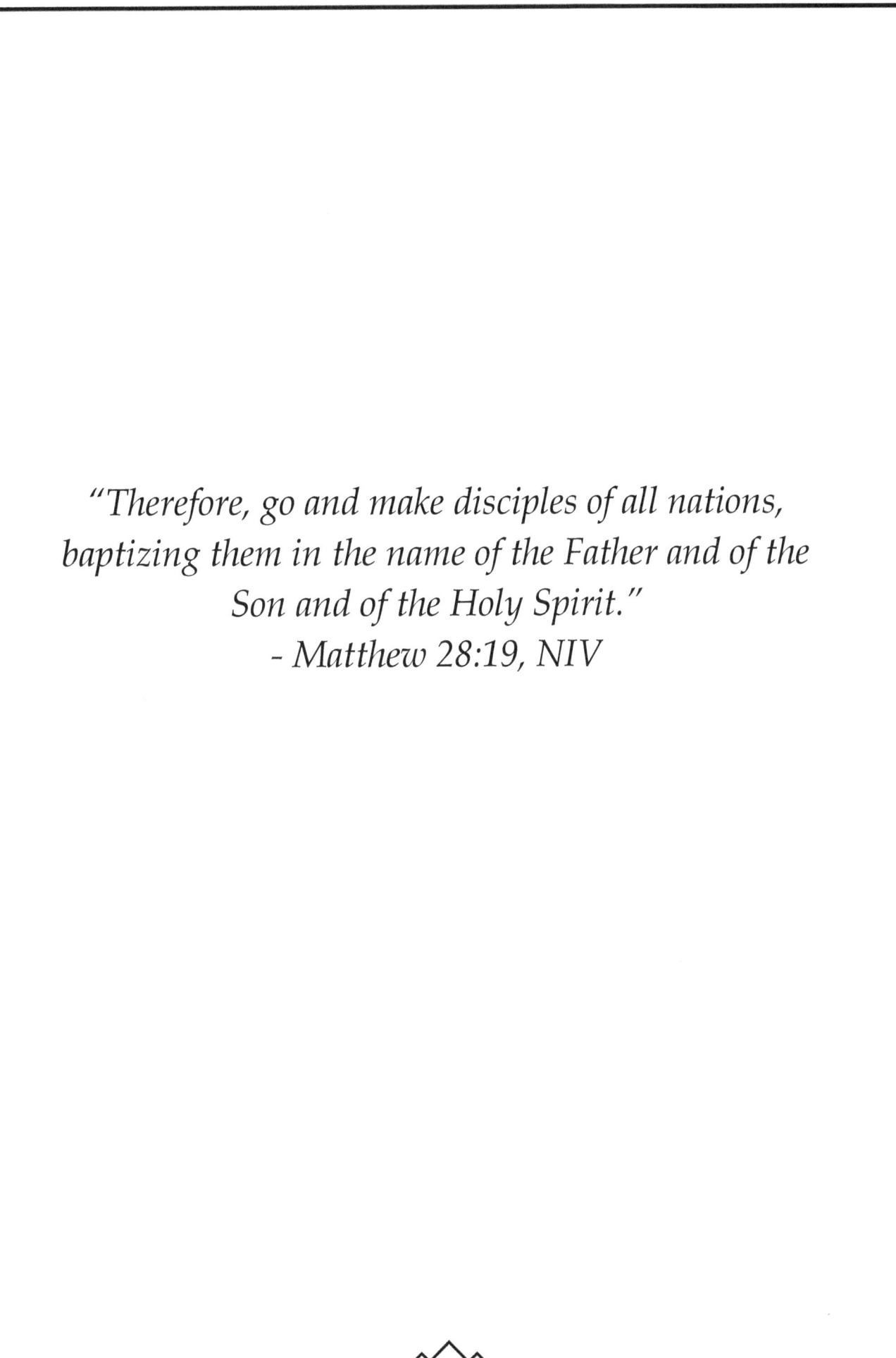

"Therefore, go and make disciples of all nations, baptizing them in the name of the Father and of the Son and of the Holy Spirit."
- Matthew 28:19, NIV

Contents

Acknowledgments

I want to thank my Heavenly Father for placing the desire in my heart to put this study together. May He receive the GLORY for any changes made in people's lives as they are going through it!

Thanks to *all* the people who encouraged me, mentored me, taught me, and helped me along the way in producing this Twelve Week Discipleship Bible Study. May God bless each one of you in a personal and powerful way!

STOP!

Before reading forward, have you completed *God Speaks, Are You Listening? Volume 1.*

If not, please don't begin this part of the study before completing Volume 1. If you haven't yet gotten your copy, go to: bwicministries.com/biblestudy, get your copy, and complete it.

Then come back and continue here.

Week Seven

Led by the Holy Spirit

---◆---

In this week, allow the Holy Spirit to lead you. Give up your agenda and be faithful to obey the Spirit's leadership. In Galatians 5:16-18, NIV *Life Application Bible* commentary (1991) states:

> Being led by the Holy Spirit involves the desire to hear, the readiness to obey God's Word, and the sensitivity to discern between your feelings and His promptings. Live each day controlled and guided by the Holy Spirit. Then the words of Christ will be in your mind, the love of Christ will be behind your actions, and the power of Christ will help you control your selfish desires.

Share with your accountability partner what the Holy Spirit may have led you to do. Did you follow through faithfully? How?

Write out your goals from last week to keep them in mind until the new habit is formed. Make any needed adjustments.

Goals	Spiritual	Mental	Social/ Emotional	Physical	Financial
New Habit (What...be specific)					
Measurable Growth (How much and/or when)					
Period (daily, weekly, monthly)					

Week Seven

Day: _____ Date: _____ Time: _____

Lesson 1: Walking in the Spirit

Scripture Reading: Galatians 5:13-18

What did you learn in today's reading? How will you apply it to your life?

_____

_____

_____

_____

_____

_____

Who may have cut in on you and kept you from obeying the truth? How did they do this? What can you do now?

_____

_____

_____

_____

_____

_____

What specific goal have you set for your Spiritual growth and refinement for this week? What is your progress?

_____

_____

Write the memory verse for this week: *Romans 8:14.*

_____

_____

_____

Write out three things you are grateful for today.

_____

_____

_____

Write out a prayer to God responding to today's lesson.

_____

_____

_____

_____

_____

_____

Ask, "Lord, what do You want to say to me personally about serving others?"

_____

_____

_____

_____

_____

_____

Reflection: How did you experience God in a special way today or yesterday?

_____

_____

_____

_____

_____

Pray for: Someone to be saved _____ someone to disciple _____

Date	Prayer Requests Received Today	How and when answered? (Come back and follow up as needed)

Week Seven

Day: _____ Date: _____ Time: _____

Lesson 2: Fruit of the Spirit

Scripture Reading: Galatians 5:19-26

What did you learn in today's reading? How will you apply it to your life?

_____

_____

_____

_____

_____

_____

Is there a sinful nature that is active in your life right now? If so, what will you do to stop that activity in your life?

_____

_____

_____

_____

_____

_____

What specific goal have you set for your Mental growth and refinement for this week? What is your progress?

_____

_____

Write the memory verse for this week: *Romans 8:14.*

_____

_____

Write out three things you are grateful for today.

_____

_____

_____

Write out a prayer to God responding to today's lesson.

_____

_____

_____

_____

_____

_____

Ask, "Lord, what do You want to say to me personally about the fruit of the Spirit in my life?"

_____

_____

_____

_____

_____

_____

_____

Reflection: How did you experience God in a special way today or yesterday?

_____

_____

_____

_____

_____

Pray for: Someone to be saved _____ someone to disciple _____

Date	Prayer Requests Received Today	How and when answered? (Come back and follow up as needed)

Week Seven

Day: _____ Date: _____ Time: _____

Scripture Reading: Gospel of John 14:1-6

What did you learn in today's reading? How will you apply it to your life?

_____

_____

_____

_____

_____

_____

After meditating on this passage, what word(s) of revelation came alive and spoke to your heart? How will you live it out?

_____

_____

_____

_____

_____

_____

_____

What specific goal have you set for your Social/Emotional growth and refinement for this week? What is your progress?

_____

_____

Write the memory verse for this week: *Romans 8:14.*

_____

_____

_____

Write out three things you are grateful for today.

_____

_____

_____

Write out a prayer to God responding to today's lesson.

_____

_____

_____

_____

_____

_____

Ask, "Lord, what do You want to say to me personally about the area of life I need to trust You with more?"

_____

_____

_____

_____

_____

_____

Reflection: How did you experience God in a special way today or yesterday?

_____

_____

_____

_____

_____

Pray for: Someone to be saved _____ someone to disciple _____

Date	Prayer Requests Received Today	How and when answered? (Come back and follow up as needed)

Week Seven

Day: _____ Date: _____ Time: _____

Scripture Reading: Gospel of John 14:7-11

What did you learn in today's reading? How will you apply it to your life?

_____

_____

_____

_____

_____

_____

What do you believe about the Father?

_____

_____

_____

_____

_____

_____

What specific goal have you set for your Physical growth and refinement for this week? What is your progress?

_____

_____

Write the memory verse for this week: *Romans 8:14.*

_____

_____

_____

Write out three things you are grateful for today.

_____

_____

_____

Write out a prayer to God responding to today's lesson.

_____

_____

_____

_____

_____

_____

Ask, "Lord, what do You want to say to me personally about how You show Yourself to me?"

_____

_____

_____

_____

_____

_____

_____

Reflection: How did you experience God in a special way today or yesterday?

_____

_____

_____

_____

_____

Pray for: Someone to be saved _____ someone to disciple _____

Date	Prayer Requests Received Today	How and when answered? (Come back and follow up as needed)

Week Seven

Day: _____ Date: _____ Time: _____

Scripture Reading: Gospel of John 14:12-14

What did you learn in today's reading? How will you apply it to your life?

_____

_____

_____

_____

_____

_____

What is God asking you to do? How will you live it out?

_____

_____

_____

_____

_____

_____

What specific goal have you set for your Financial growth and refinement for this week? What is your progress?

_____

_____

Write the memory verse for this week: *Romans 8:14.*

_____

_____

_____

Write out three things you are grateful for today.

_____

_____

_____

Write out a prayer to God responding to today's lesson.

_____

_____

_____

_____

_____

_____

Ask, "Lord, what do You want to say to me personally about the things I ask of You to do?"

_____

_____

_____

_____

_____

_____

Reflection: How did you experience God in a special way today or yesterday?

_____

_____

_____

_____

_____

Pray for: Someone to be saved _____ someone to disciple _____

Date	Prayer Requests Received Today	How and when answered? (Come back and follow up as needed)

Notes

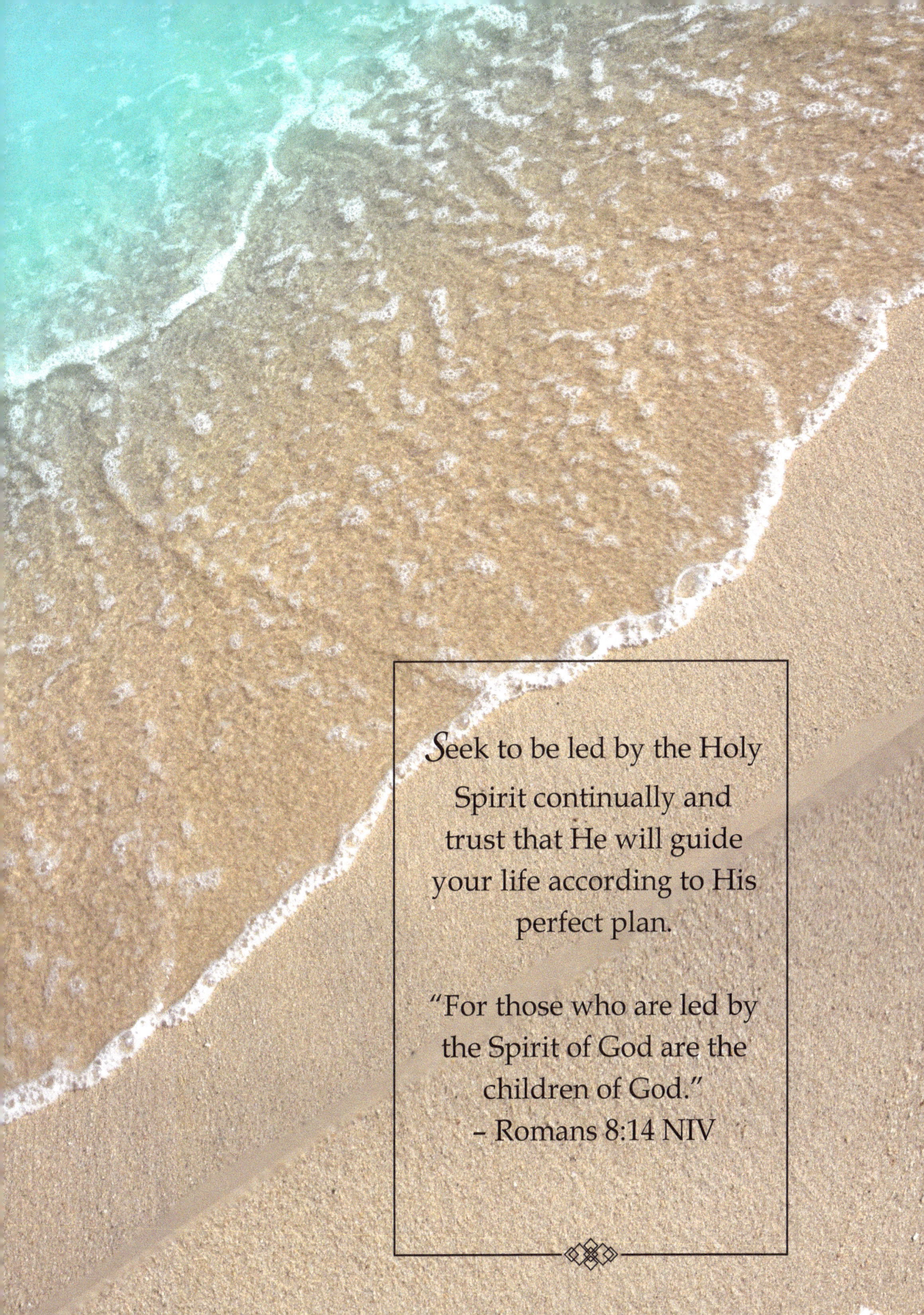

Seek to be led by the Holy
Spirit continually and
trust that He will guide
your life according to His
perfect plan.

"For those who are led by
the Spirit of God are the
children of God."
– Romans 8:14 NIV

Church Sermon Notes

Theme:

_____

_____

_____

Scriptures:

_____

_____

_____

Lessons:

_____

_____

_____

_____

_____

_____

Application:

_____

_____

_____

_____

_____

_____

Notes:

_____

_____

_____

_____

_____

Things to Remember from Week Seven

———————◆———————

Scriptures:

_____

_____

_____

Application:

_____

_____

_____

Goals Set:

_____

_____

_____

Memory Verse:

_____

_____

_____

Time with God:

_____

_____

_____

Reflection:

_____

_____

_____

Answered Prayers:

_____

_____

_____

Week Eight

Trust & Believe

---◆---

In this week, trust and believe in the Holy Spirit's leadership. He may reveal something that does not seem possible. However, with God, all things are possible.

Share with your accountability partner what the Holy Spirit may have led you to do. Was your faith evaluated to let God lead in this situation or direction? How?

_____

_____

_____

_____

_____

_____

Write out your goals from last week to keep them in mind until the new habit is formed. Make any needed adjustments.

Goals	Spiritual	Mental	Social/ Emotional	Physical	Financial
New Habit (What…be specific)					
Measurable Growth (How much and/or when)					
Period (daily, weekly, monthly)					

Week Eight

Day: _____ Date: _____ Time: _____

Lesson 1: Jesus Promises…

Scripture Reading: Gospel of John 14:15-18

What did you learn in today's reading? How will you apply it to your life?

_____

_____

_____

_____

_____

_____

How are you showing that you love Jesus?

_____

_____

_____

_____

_____

What specific goal have you set for your Spiritual growth and refinement for this week? What is your progress?

_____

_____

Write the memory verse for this week: *Proverbs 3:5-6.*

_____

_____

_____

_____

Write out three things you are grateful for today.

_____

_____

_____

Write out a prayer to God responding to today's lesson.

_____

_____

_____

_____

_____

_____

Ask, "Lord, what do You want to say to me personally about the way I obey Your commands?"

_____

_____

_____

_____

_____

_____

Reflection: How did you experience God in a special way today or yesterday?

_____

_____

_____

_____

_____

Pray for: Someone to be saved _____ someone to disciple _____

Date	Prayer Requests Received Today	How and when answered? (Come back and follow up as needed)

Week Eight

Day: _____ Date: _____ Time: _____

Lesson 2: Indwelling

Scripture Reading: Gospel of John 14:19-24

What did you learn in today's reading? How will you apply it to your life?

_____

_____

_____

_____

_____

_____

How will Jesus show Himself to you?

_____

_____

_____

_____

_____

_____

What specific goal have you set for your Mental growth and refinement for this week? What is your progress?

_____

_____

Write the memory verse for this week: *Proverbs 3:5-6.*

_____

_____

_____

_____

Write out three things you are grateful for today.

_____

_____

_____

Write out a prayer to God responding to today's lesson.

_____

_____

_____

_____

_____

_____

_____

Ask, "Lord, what do You want to say to me personally about how You show Yourself to me?"

_____

_____

_____

_____

_____

_____

_____

_____

Reflection: How did you experience God in a special way today or yesterday?

_____

_____

_____

_____

_____

_____

Pray for: Someone to be saved _____ someone to disciple _____

Date	Prayer Requests Received Today	How and when answered? (Come back and follow up as needed)

Week Eight

Day: _____ Date: _____ Time: _____

Lesson 3: Gift of Peace

Scripture Reading: Gospel of John 14:25-31

What did you learn in today's reading? How will you apply it to your life?

_____

_____

_____

_____

_____

After meditating on this passage, what word(s) of revelation came alive and spoke to your heart? How will you live it out?

_____

_____

_____

_____

_____

_____

What specific goal have you set for your Social/Emotional growth and refinement for this week? What is your progress?

_____

_____

Write the memory verse for this week: *Proverbs 3:5-6.*

_____

_____

_____

_____

Write out three things you are grateful for today.

_____

_____

_____

Write out a prayer to God responding to today's lesson.

_____

_____

_____

_____

_____

_____

Ask, "Lord, what do You want to say to me personally about how to receive peace in my life?"

_____

_____

_____

_____

_____

_____

_____

Reflection: How did you experience God in a special way today or yesterday?

_____

_____

_____

_____

_____

Pray for: Someone to be saved _____ someone to disciple _____

Date	Prayer Requests Received Today	How and when answered? (Come back and follow up as needed)

Week Eight

Day: _____ Date: _____ Time: _____

Lesson 4: The True Vine

Scripture Reading: Gospel of John 15:1-8

What did you learn in today's reading? How will you apply it to your life?

_____

_____

_____

_____

_____

_____

How are you staying connected to the vine?

_____

_____

_____

_____

_____

_____

What specific goal have you set for your Physical growth and refinement for this week? What is your progress?

_____

_____

Write the memory verse for this week: *Proverbs 3:5-6.*

_____

_____

_____

_____

Write out three things you are grateful for today.

_____

_____

_____

Write out a prayer to God responding to today's lesson.

_____

_____

_____

_____

_____

_____

Ask, "Lord, what do You want to say to me personally about being connected to the vine?"

_____

_____

_____

_____

_____

_____

Reflection: How did you experience God in a special way today or yesterday?

_____

_____

_____

_____

Pray for: Someone to be saved _____ someone to disciple _____

Date	Prayer Requests Received Today	How and when answered? (Come back and follow up as needed)

Week Eight

Day: _____ Date: _____ Time: _____

Lesson 5: Love and Joy

Scripture Reading: Gospel of John 15:9-17

What did you learn in today's reading? How will you apply it to your life?

_____

_____

_____

_____

_____

_____

How can you develop joy in your heart?

_____

_____

_____

_____

_____

What specific goal have you set for your Financial growth and refinement for this week? What is your progress?

_____

_____

_____

Write the memory verse for this week: *Proverbs 3:5-6.*

_____

_____

_____

_____

Write out three things you are grateful for today.

_____

_____

_____

Write out a prayer to God responding to today's lesson.

_____

_____

_____

_____

_____

_____

Ask, "Lord, what do You want to say to me personally about the kind of fruit that will last?"

_____

_____

_____

_____

_____

_____

Reflection: How did you experience God in a special way today or yesterday?

_____

_____

_____

_____

_____

Pray for: Someone to be saved _____ someone to disciple _____

Date	Prayer Requests Received Today	How and when answered? (Come back and follow up as needed)

Notes

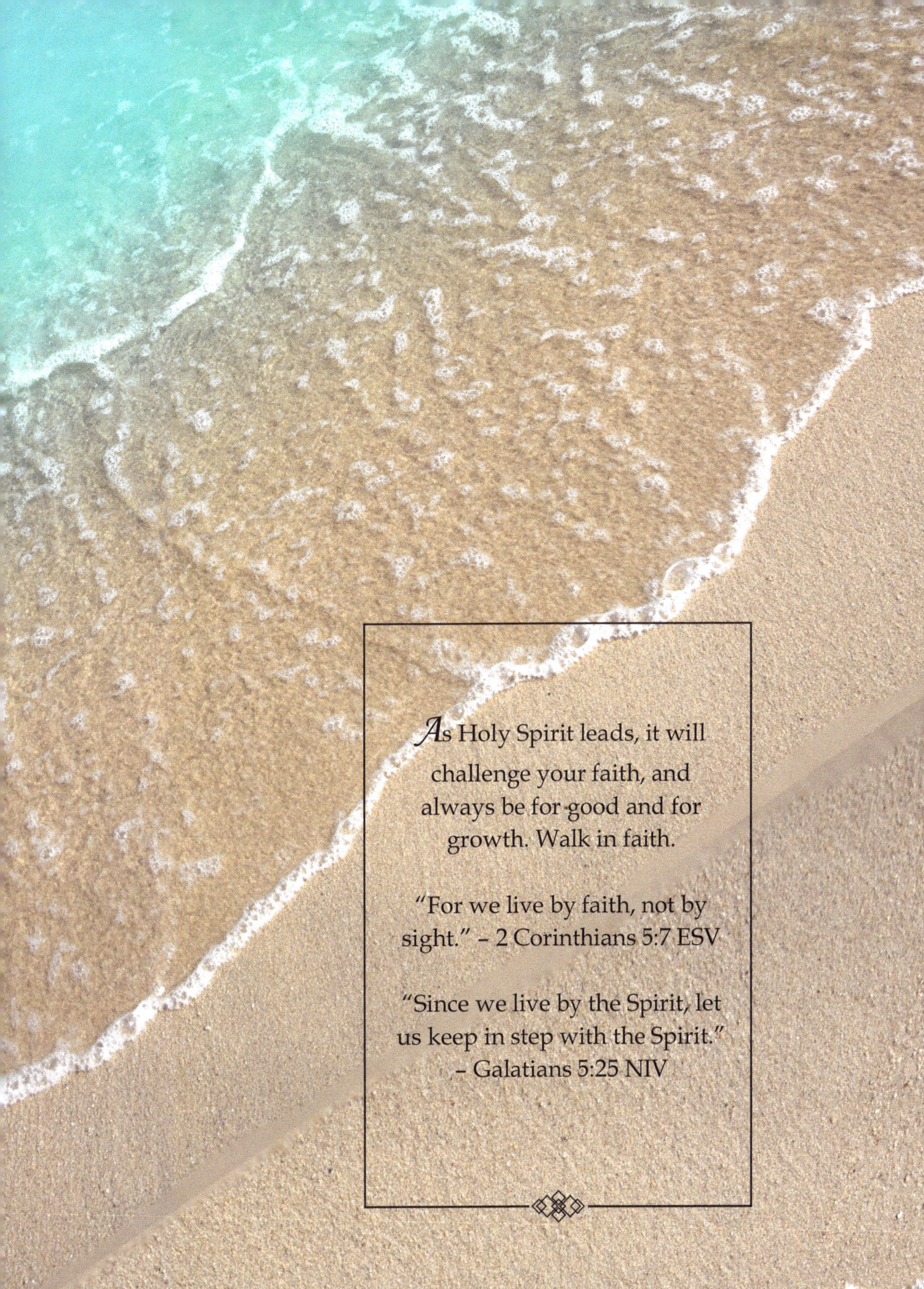

*A*s Holy Spirit leads, it will challenge your faith, and always be for good and for growth. Walk in faith.

"For we live by faith, not by sight." – 2 Corinthians 5:7 ESV

"Since we live by the Spirit, let us keep in step with the Spirit." – Galatians 5:25 NIV

Church Sermon Notes

Theme:

_____

_____

_____

Scriptures:

_____

_____

_____

Lessons:

_____

_____

_____

_____

_____

_____

Application:

_____

_____

_____

_____

_____

_____

Notes:

_____

_____

_____

_____

_____

_____

Things to Remember from Week Eight

———◆———

Scriptures:

_____

_____

_____

Application:

_____

_____

_____

Goals Set:

_____

_____

_____

Memory Verse:

_____

_____

_____

Time with God:

_____

_____

_____

Reflection:

_____

_____

_____

Answered Prayers:

_____

_____

_____

Week Nine

Receiving Answers

———— ◆ ————

Are you starting to see more changes in your life? In this week, be prepared to start receiving answers to your challenges. God may bring a person into your life that will help you achieve your goals. Share with your accountability/prayer partner any answers to your challenges.

Write out your goals from last week to keep them in mind until the new habit is formed. Make any needed adjustments.

Goals	Spiritual	Mental	Social/ Emotional	Physical	Financial
New Habit (What…be specific)					
Measurable Growth (How much and/or when)					
Period (daily, weekly, monthly)					

Week Nine

Day: _____ Date: _____ Time: _____

Lesson 1: World's Hatred

Scripture Reading: Gospel of John 15:18-25

What did you learn in today's reading? How will you apply it to your life?

_____

_____

_____

_____

_____

_____

Have you ever felt like you were hated by those around you? What did you do about it?

_____

_____

_____

_____

_____

_____

What specific goal have you set for your Spiritual growth and refinement for this week? What is your progress?

_____

_____

Write the memory verse for this week: *John 16:24.*

_____

_____

_____

Write out three things you are grateful for today

_____

_____

_____

Write out a prayer to God responding to today's lesson.

_____
_____
_____
_____
_____
_____
_____

Ask, "Lord, what do You want to say to me personally about being persecuted?"

_____
_____
_____
_____
_____
_____
_____

Reflection: How did you experience God in a special way today or yesterday?

_____
_____
_____
_____
_____
_____

Pray for: Someone to be saved _____ someone to disciple _____

Date	Prayer Requests Received Today	How and when answered? (Come back and follow up as needed)

Week Nine

Day: _____ Date: _____ Time: _____

Scripture Reading: Gospel of John 15:26-16:4

What did you learn in today's reading? How will you apply it to your life?

_____

_____

_____

_____

_____

_____

How do you testify about Jesus?

_____

_____

_____

_____

_____

_____

What specific goal have you set for your Mental growth and refinement for this week? What is your progress?

_____

_____

Write the memory verse for this week: *John 16:24.*

_____

_____

_____

Write out three things you are grateful for today.

_____

_____

_____

Write out a prayer to God responding to today's lesson.

_____

_____

_____

_____

_____

_____

Ask, "Lord, what do You want to say to me personally about the Spirit of truth?"

_____

_____

_____

_____

_____

_____

_____

Reflection: How did you experience God in a special way today or yesterday?

_____

_____

_____

_____

_____

Pray for: Someone to be saved _____ someone to disciple _____

Date	Prayer Requests Received Today	How and when answered? (Come back and follow up as needed)

Week Nine

Day: _____ Date: _____ Time: _____

Lesson 3: Holy Spirit

Scripture Reading: Gospel of John 16:5-15

What did you learn in today's reading? How will you apply it to your life?

_____

_____

_____

_____

_____

_____

Is the Holy Spirit convicting you of guilt, sin, or righteousness? What can you do to make a change in your life?

_____

_____

_____

_____

_____

_____

What specific goal have you set for your Social/Emotional growth and refinement for this week? What is your progress?

_____

_____

Write the memory verse for this week: *John 16:24.*

_____

_____

_____

Write out three things you are grateful for today.

_____

_____

_____

Write out a prayer to God responding to today's lesson.

_____

_____

_____

_____

_____

_____

Ask, "Lord, what do You want to say to me personally about belonging to You?"

_____

_____

_____

_____

_____

_____

_____

Reflection: How did you experience God in a special way today or yesterday?

_____

_____

_____

_____

_____

Pray for: Someone to be saved _____ someone to disciple _____

Date	Prayer Requests Received Today	How and when answered? (Come back and follow up as needed)

Week Nine

Day: _____ Date: _____ Time: _____

Lesson 4: Sorrow Turned to Joy

Scripture Reading: Gospel of John 16:16-24

What did you learn in today's reading? How will you apply it to your life?

_____

_____

_____

_____

_____

_____

After meditating on this passage, what must change in your life, so you are living as God wants? How will you live it out?

_____

_____

_____

_____

_____

_____

What specific goal have you set for your Physical growth and refinement for this week? What is your progress?

_____

_____

Write the memory verse for this week: *John 16:24.*

_____

_____

_____

Write out three things you are grateful for today.

_____

_____

_____

Write out a prayer to God responding to today's lesson.

_____

_____

_____

_____

_____

_____

Ask, "Lord, what do You want to say to me personally about how to have joy in my life, no matter my circumstances?"

_____

_____

_____

_____

_____

_____

Reflection: How did you experience God in a special way today or yesterday?

_____

_____

_____

_____

_____

Pray for: Someone to be saved _____ someone to disciple _____

Date	Prayer Requests Received Today	How and when answered? (Come back and follow up as needed)

Week Nine

Day: _____ Date: _____ Time: _____

Lesson 5: Jesus Overcomes

Scripture Reading: Gospel of John 16:25-33

What did you learn in today's reading? How will you apply it to your life?

_____

_____

_____

_____

_____

_____

What area in your life are you trying to overcome? Have you given it over to Jesus?

_____

_____

_____

_____

_____

_____

What specific goal have you set for your Financial growth and refinement for this week? What is your progress?

_____

_____

Write the memory verse for this week: *John 16:24*.

_____

_____

_____

Write out three things you are grateful for today.

_____

_____

_____

Write out a prayer to God responding to today's lesson.

_____

_____

_____

_____

_____

_____

Ask, "Lord, what do You want to say to me personally about overcoming with victory?"

_____

_____

_____

_____

_____

_____

_____

Reflection: How did you experience God in a special way today or yesterday?

_____

_____

_____

_____

Pray for: Someone to be saved _____ someone to disciple _____

Date	Prayer Requests Received Today	How and when answered? (Come back and follow up as needed)

Notes

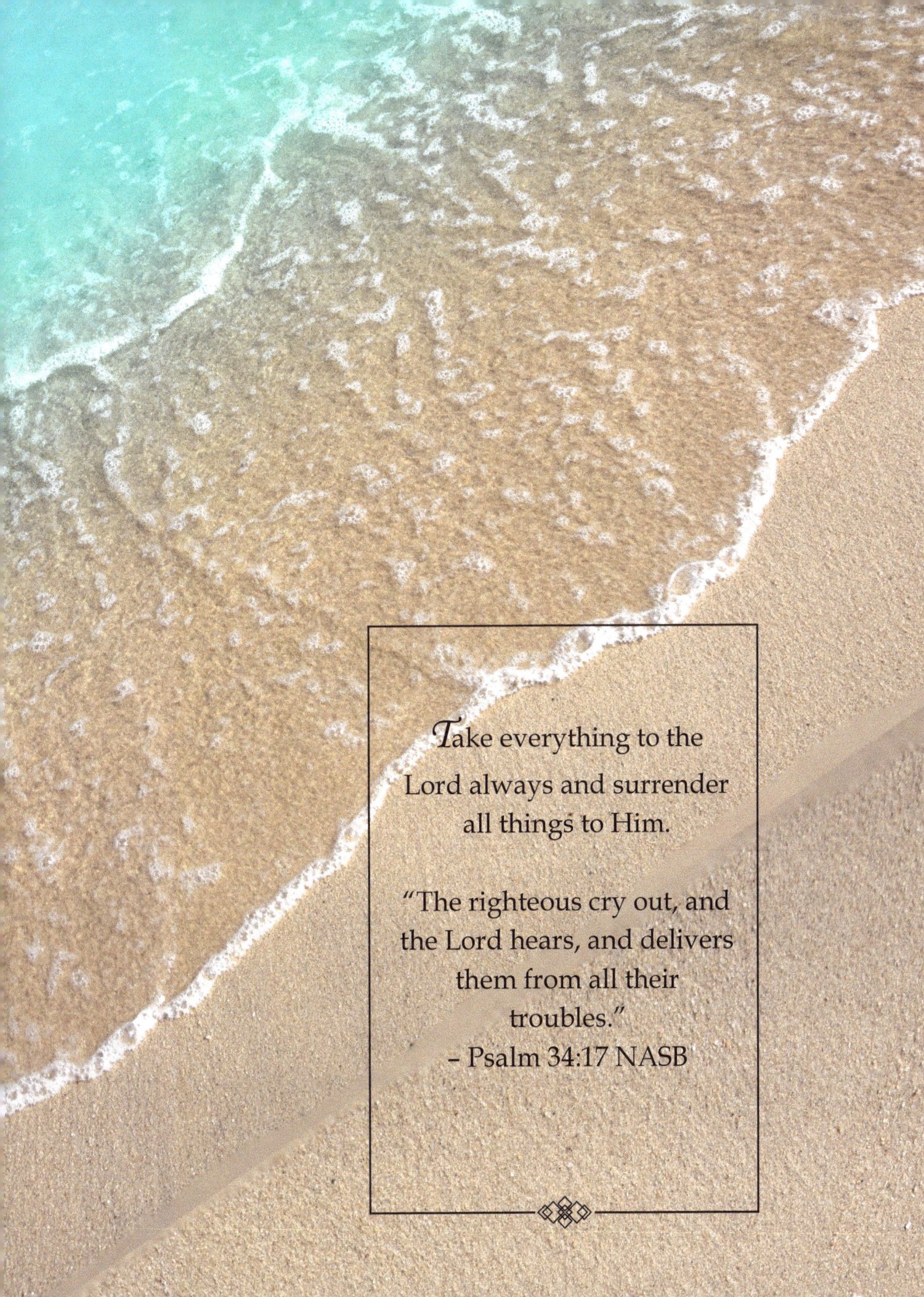

*T*ake everything to the
Lord always and surrender
all things to Him.

"The righteous cry out, and
the Lord hears, and delivers
them from all their
troubles."
– Psalm 34:17 NASB

Church Sermon Notes

Theme:

_____

_____

_____

Scriptures:

_____

_____

_____

Lessons:

_____

_____

_____

_____

_____

_____

Application:

_____

_____

_____

_____

_____

_____

Notes:

_____

_____

_____

_____

_____

Things to Remember from Week Nine

————◆————

Scriptures:

_____

_____

_____

Application:

_____

_____

_____

Goals Set:

_____

_____

_____

Memory Verse:

_____

_____

_____

Time with God:

_____

_____

_____

Reflection:

_____

_____

_____

Answered Prayers:

_____

_____

_____

Week Ten

Pray Continually

———◆———

This week challenges you to pray more. In I Thessalonians 5:17, it says, "Pray continually."

Continue to lift your challenges, anxieties, or struggles to God in prayer, and thank Him for what He has been doing so far in your life. May He receive the glory! ☺ Share with your accountability partner any prayer requests that still need to be answered. Take time to pray together more intensely, specifically, and intentionally.

Write out your goals from last week to keep them in mind until the new habit is formed. Make any needed adjustments.

Goals	Spiritual	Mental	Social/ Emotional	Physical	Financial
New Habit (What…be specific)					
Measurable Growth (How much and/or when)					
Period (daily, weekly, monthly)					

Week Ten

Day: _____ Date: _____ Time: _____

Lesson 1: Jesus Prays for Himself

Scripture Reading: Gospel of John 17:1-5

What did you learn in today's reading? How will you apply it to your life?

_____

_____

_____

_____

_____

Do you know the One true God and Jesus whom He sent? What do you know about them?

_____

_____

_____

_____

_____

What specific goal have you set for your Spiritual growth and refinement for this week? What is your progress?

_____

_____

Write the memory verse for this week: *I John 5:14-15,*

_____

_____

_____

_____

_____

_____

Write out three things you are grateful for today.

_____

_____

_____

Write out a prayer to God responding to today's lesson.

_____
_____
_____
_____
_____
_____

Ask, "Lord, what do You want to say to me personally about bringing glory to Your name?"

_____
_____
_____
_____
_____
_____

Reflection: How did you experience God in a special way today or yesterday?

_____
_____
_____
_____
_____

Pray for: Someone to be saved _____ someone to disciple _____

Date	Prayer Requests Received Today	How and when answered? (Come back and follow up as needed)

Week Ten

Day: _____ Date: _____ Time: _____

Lesson 2: Jesus Prays for Disciples

Scripture Reading: Gospel of John 17:6-19

What did you learn in today's reading? How will you apply it to your life?

_____

_____

_____

_____

_____

_____

Does your life reveal Jesus' character and presence? How or why not?

_____

_____

_____

_____

_____

What specific goal have you set for your Mental growth and refinement for this week? What is your progress?

_____

_____

Write the memory verse for this week: *I John 5:14-15.*

_____

_____

_____

_____

_____

_____

Write out three things you are grateful for today.

_____

_____

_____

Write out a prayer to God responding to today's lesson.

_____

_____

_____

_____

_____

_____

Ask, "Lord, what do You want to say to me personally about being sanctified?"

_____

_____

_____

_____

_____

_____

_____

Reflection: How did you experience God in a special way today or yesterday?

_____

_____

_____

_____

_____

Pray for: Someone to be saved _____ someone to disciple _____

Date	Prayer Requests Received Today	How and when answered? (Come back and follow up as needed)

Week Ten

Day: _____ Date: _____ Time: _____

Lesson 3: Jesus Prays for All Believers

Scripture Reading: Gospel of John 17:20-26

What did you learn in today's reading? How will you apply it to your life?

_____

_____

_____

_____

_____

_____

How are you helping to unify the body of Christ?

_____

_____

_____

_____

_____

What specific goal have you set for your Social/Emotional growth and refinement for this week? What is your progress?

_____

_____

Write the memory verse for this week: *1 John 5:14-15.*

_____

_____

_____

_____

_____

_____

Write out three things you are grateful for today.

_____

_____

_____

Write out a prayer to God responding to today's lesson.

_____

_____

_____

_____

_____

_____

Ask, "Lord, what do You want to say to me personally about praying for other believers?"

_____

_____

_____

_____

_____

_____

Reflection: How did you experience God in a special way today or yesterday?

_____

_____

_____

_____

_____

Pray for: Someone to be saved _____ someone to disciple _____

Date	Prayer Requests Received Today	How and when answered? (Come back and follow up as needed)

Week Ten

Day: _____ Date: _____ Time: _____

Lesson 4: Alive to God

Scripture Reading: Romans 6:1-15

What did you learn in today's reading? How will you apply it to your life?

_____

_____

_____

_____

_____

How are you offering yourself as a living sacrifice to God?

_____

_____

_____

_____

_____

What specific goal have you set for your Physical growth and refinement for this week? What is your progress?

_____

_____

Write the memory verse for this week: *I John 5:14-15.*

_____

_____

_____

_____

_____

_____

Write out three things you are grateful for today.

_____

_____

_____

Write out a prayer to God responding to today's lesson.

_____

_____

_____

_____

_____

_____

Ask, "Lord, what do You want to say to me personally about being alive in You?"

_____

_____

_____

_____

_____

_____

Reflection: How did you experience God in a special way today or yesterday?

_____

_____

_____

_____

_____

Pray for: Someone to be saved _____ someone to disciple _____

Date	Prayer Requests Received Today	How and when answered? (Come back and follow up as needed)

Week Ten

Day: _____ Date: _____ Time: _____

Scripture Reading: Romans 6:16-23

What did you learn in today's reading? How will you apply it to your life?

_____

_____

_____

_____

_____

Are you serving your sinful nature or serving God? How do you rate your heart of obedience? Is it fully committed to God or half-hardheartedly serving Him?

_____

_____

_____

_____

_____

_____

What specific goal have you set for your Financial growth and refinement for this week? What is your progress?

_____

_____

Write the memory verse for this week: *I John 5:14-15.*

_____

_____

_____

_____

_____

_____

Write out three things you are grateful for today.

_____

_____

_____

Write out a prayer to God responding to today's lesson.

_____

_____

_____

_____

_____

_____

Ask, "Lord, what do You want to say to me personally about being fully committed to You?"

_____

_____

_____

_____

_____

_____

_____

Reflection: How did you experience God in a special way today or yesterday?

_____

_____

_____

_____

_____

Pray for: Someone to be saved _____ someone to disciple _____

Date	Prayer Requests Received Today	How and when answered? (Come back and follow up as needed)

Notes

The more you pray, the more you will see the hand of God in your life. So pray continuously every day.

"Give all your worries to Him because He cares for you." – 1 Peter 5:7 NLV

Church Sermon Notes

———————◆———————

Theme:

_____

_____

_____

Scriptures:

_____

_____

_____

Lessons:

_____

_____

_____

_____

_____

_____

Application:

_____

_____

_____

_____

_____

_____

Notes:

_____

_____

_____

_____

_____

Things to Remember from Week Ten

———◆———

Scriptures:

_____

_____

_____

Application:

_____

_____

_____

Goals Set:

_____

_____

_____

Memory Verse:

_____

_____

_____

Time with God:

_____

_____

_____

Reflection:

_____

_____

_____

Answered Prayers:

_____

_____

_____

Week Eleven

Open Mind & Heart

—◆—

"Do not conform to the pattern of this world but be transformed by the renewing of your mind. Then you will be able to test and approve what God's will is — His good, pleasing and perfect will." Romans 12:2

This week you may see how God can place things in your life that reflect your change. Keep an open mind and heart to this change. Continue to lift your challenges, anxieties, or struggles to God in prayer, and thank Him for what He has been doing in your life. May He receive the glory! ☺ Share with your accountability partner anything God has revealed to you specifically.

Write out your goals from last week to keep them in mind until the new habit is formed. Make any needed adjustments.

Goals	Spiritual	Mental	Social/ Emotional	Physical	Financial
New Habit (What…be specific)					
Measurable Growth (How much and/or when)					
Period (daily, weekly, monthly)					

Week Eleven

Day: _____ Date: _____ Time: _____

Lesson 1: Life through the Spirit

Scripture Reading: Romans 8:1-11

What did you learn in today's reading? How will you apply it to your life?

_____

_____

_____

_____

_____

_____

Do you have your mind set on sinful nature or the Spirit? What can you do to be more Spirit-minded?

_____

_____

_____

_____

_____

_____

What specific goal have you set for your Spiritual growth and refinement for this week? What is your progress?

_____

_____

Write the memory verse for this week: *Romans 12:2.*

_____

_____

_____

Write out three things you are grateful for today.

_____

_____

_____

Write out a prayer to God responding to today's lesson.

_____

_____

_____

_____

_____

_____

Ask, "Lord, what do You want to say to me personally about where my focus needs to be?"

_____

_____

_____

_____

_____

_____

Reflection: How did you experience God in a special way today or yesterday?

_____

_____

_____

_____

_____

Pray for: Someone to be saved _____ someone to disciple _____

Date	Prayer Requests Received Today	How and when answered? (Come back and follow up as needed)

Week Eleven

Day: _____ Date: _____ Time: _____

Lesson 2: Adoption

Scripture Reading: Romans 8:12-17

What did you learn in today's reading? How will you apply it to your life?

_____

_____

_____

_____

_____

_____

_____

Have you been adopted into the family of God? How will you cherish this blessing?

_____

_____

_____

_____

_____

_____

What specific goal have you set for your Mental growth and references for this week? What is your progress?

_____

_____

Write the memory verse for this week: *Romans 12:2.*

_____

_____

_____

Write out three things you are grateful for today.

_____

_____

_____

Write out a prayer to God responding to today's lesson.

_____

_____

_____

_____

_____

Ask, "Lord, what do You want to say to me personally about being Your heir?"

_____

_____

_____

_____

_____

_____

Reflection: How did you experience God in a special way today or yesterday?

_____

_____

_____

_____

Pray for: Someone to be saved _____ someone to disciple _____

Date	Prayer Requests Received Today	How and when answered? (Come back and follow up as needed)

Week Eleven

Day: _____ Date: _____ Time: _____

Lesson 3: Suffering to Glory

Scripture Reading: Romans 8:18-30

What did you learn in today's reading? How will you apply it to your life?

_____

_____

_____

_____

_____

_____

What things can you do to be conformed into Christ-likeness?

_____

_____

_____

_____

_____

What specific goal have you set for your Social/Emotional growth and refinement for this week? What is your progress?

_____

_____

Write the memory verse for this week: *Romans 12:2.*

_____

_____

_____

Write out three things you are grateful for today.

_____

_____

_____

Write out a prayer to God responding to today's lesson.

_____

_____

_____

_____

_____

_____

Ask, "Lord, what do You want to say to me personally about being conformed into the image of Christ?"

_____

_____

_____

_____

_____

_____

_____

Reflection: How did you experience God in a special way today or yesterday?

_____

_____

_____

_____

_____

Pray for: Someone to be saved _____ someone to disciple _____

Date	Prayer Requests Received Today	How and when answered? (Come back and follow up as needed)

Week Eleven

Day: _____ Date: _____ Time: _____

Lesson 4: Everlasting Love

Scripture Reading: Romans 8:31-39

What did you learn in today's reading? How will you apply it to your life?

_____

_____

_____

_____

_____

_____

How are you more than a conqueror?

_____

_____

_____

_____

_____

_____

What specific goal have you set for your Physical growth and refinement for this week? What is your progress?

_____

_____

Write the memory verse for this week: *Romans 12:2.*

_____

_____

_____

Write out three things you are grateful for today.

_____

_____

_____

Write out a prayer to God responding to today's lesson.

_____

_____

_____

_____

_____

_____

Ask, "Lord, what do You want to say to me personally about Your love for me?"

_____

_____

_____

_____

_____

_____

_____

Reflection: How did you experience God in a special way today or yesterday?

_____

_____

_____

_____

_____

Pray for: Someone to be saved _____ someone to disciple _____

Date	Prayer Requests Received Today	How and when answered? (Come back and follow up as needed)

Week Eleven

Day: _____ Date: _____ Time: _____

Scripture Reading: Romans 12:1-2

What did you learn in today's reading? How will you apply it to your life?

_____

_____

_____

_____

_____

_____

Are you being transformed in your mind? If so, what changes have you made?

_____

_____

_____

_____

_____

_____

What specific goal have you set for your Financial growth and refinement for this week? What is your progress?

_____

_____

Write the memory verse for this week: *Romans 12:2.*

_____

_____

_____

Write out three things you are grateful for today.

_____

_____

_____

Write out a prayer to God responding to today's lesson.

_____

_____

_____

_____

_____

Ask, "Lord, what do You want to say to me personally about the renewing of the mind?"

_____

_____

_____

_____

_____

_____

Reflection: How did you experience God in a special way today or yesterday?

_____

_____

_____

_____

Pray for: Someone to be saved _____ someone to disciple _____

Date	Prayer Requests Received Today	How and when answered? (Come back and follow up as needed)

Notes

$\mathcal{P}$ray and seek out the mind of Christ, and you will have peace, hope, joy, and love.

"Finally, brothers and sisters, whatever is true, whatever is noble, whatever is right, whatever is pure, whatever is lovely, whatever is admirable—if anything is excellent or praiseworthy— think about such things."
– Philippians 4:8 NIV

Church Sermon Notes

Theme:

_____
_____
_____

Scriptures:

_____
_____
_____

Lessons:

_____
_____
_____
_____
_____
_____

Application:

_____
_____
_____
_____
_____
_____

Notes:

_____
_____
_____
_____
_____

Things to Remember from Week Eleven

Scriptures:

_____

_____

_____

Application:

_____

_____

_____

Goals Set:

_____

_____

_____

Memory Verse:

_____

_____

_____

Time with God:

_____

_____

_____

Reflection:

_____

_____

_____

Answered Prayers:

_____

_____

_____

Week Twelve

Breakthrough

———— ◆ ————

In this week, be prepared for breakthroughs with your challenges if you haven't already been experiencing them. It may be difficult for you to do, but perseverance has its rewards. **At the end of this study, you will find a final self-evaluation form. Please take time to fill out and notice the changes that have taken place in your life from your first self-evaluation.** Share with your accountability partner all the changes you have seen take place in your life.

Write out your goals from last week to keep them in mind until the new habit is formed. Make any needed adjustments.

Goals	Spiritual	Mental	Social/ Emotional	Physical	Financial
New Habit (What…be specific)					
Measurable Growth (How much and/or when)					
Period (daily, weekly, monthly)					

Week Twelve

Day: _____ Date: _____ Time: _____

Lesson 1: Spiritual Gifts

Scripture Reading: Romans 12:3-8

What did you learn in today's reading? How will you apply it to your life?

_____

_____

_____

_____

_____

Do you know what spiritual gifts God has placed within you? How are you using them for His glory? (Reference Week 5 as needed; consider what the Lord has revealed and worked in you over the last 12 weeks.)

_____

_____

_____

_____

_____

_____

What specific goal have you set for your Spiritual growth and refinement for this week? What is your progress?

_____

_____

Write the memory verse for this week: *1 Corinthians 15:57.*

_____

_____

_____

Write out three things you are grateful for today.

_____

_____

_____

Write out a prayer to God responding to today's lesson.

_____

_____

_____

_____

_____

_____

Ask, "Lord, what do You want to say to me personally about the gifts You have placed in me?"

_____

_____

_____

_____

_____

_____

Reflection: How did you experience God in a special way today or yesterday?

_____

_____

_____

_____

_____

Pray for: Someone to be saved _____ someone to disciple _____

Date	Prayer Requests Received Today	How and when answered? (Come back and follow up as needed)

Week Twelve

Day: _____ Date: _____ Time: _____

Lesson 2: Sincere Love

Scripture Reading: Romans 12:9-21

What did you learn in today's reading? How will you apply it to your life?

_____

_____

_____

_____

_____

_____

How are you showing love in action?

_____

_____

_____

_____

_____

What specific goal have you set for your Mental growth and refinement for this week? What is your progress?

_____

_____

Write the memory verse for this week: *1 Corinthians 15:57.*

_____

_____

_____

Write out three things you are grateful for today.

_____

_____

_____

Write out a prayer to God responding to today's lesson.

_____

_____

_____

_____

_____

_____

_____

Ask, "Lord, what do You want to say to me personally about putting sincere love in action?"

_____

_____

_____

_____

_____

_____

Reflection: How did you experience God in a special way today or yesterday?

_____

_____

_____

_____

_____

Pray for: Someone to be saved _____ someone to disciple _____

Date	Prayer Requests Received Today	How and when answered? (Come back and follow up as needed)

Week Twelve

Day: _____ Date: _____ Time: _____

Scripture Reading: I Corinthians 13:1-3

What did you learn in today's reading? How will you apply it to your life?

_____

_____

_____

_____

_____

_____

What must change in your life so that you are living as God wants?

_____

_____

_____

_____

_____

_____

What specific goal have you set for your Social/Emotional growth and refinement for this week? What is your progress?

_____

_____

Write the memory verse for this week: *1 Corinthians 15:57.*

_____

_____

_____

Write out three things you are grateful for today.

_____

_____

_____

Write out a prayer to God responding to today's lesson.

_____

_____

_____

_____

_____

_____

Ask, "Lord, what do You want to say to me personally about living out the most excellent way?"

_____

_____

_____

_____

_____

_____

Reflection: How did you experience God in a special way today or yesterday?

_____

_____

_____

_____

_____

Pray for: Someone to be saved _____ someone to disciple _____

Date	Prayer Requests Received Today	How and when answered? (Come back and follow up as needed)

Week Twelve

Day: _____ Date: _____ Time: _____

Lesson 4: Love is...

Scripture Reading: I Corinthians 13:4-8a.

What did you learn in today's reading? How will you apply it to your life?

_____

_____

_____

_____

_____

_____

What area of love must change in your life, so you are living as God wants? How will you show it in your actions?

_____

_____

_____

_____

_____

_____

What specific goal have you set for your Physical growth and refinement for this week? What is your progress?

_____

_____

Write the memory verse for this week: *1 Corinthians 15:57.*

_____

_____

_____

Write out three things you are grateful for today.

_____

_____

_____

Write out a prayer to God responding to today's lesson.

_____

_____

_____

_____

_____

_____

Ask, "Lord, what do You want to say to me personally about love?"

_____

_____

_____

_____

_____

_____

Reflection: How did you experience God in a special way today or yesterday?

_____

_____

_____

_____

_____

Pray for: Someone to be saved _____ someone to disciple _____

Date	Prayer Requests Received Today	How and when answered? (Come back and follow up as needed)

Week Twelve

Day: _____ Date: _____ Time: _____

Lesson 5: Faith, Hope, & Love

Scripture Reading: I Corinthians 13:4b-13.

What did you learn in today's reading? How will you apply it to your life?

_____

_____

_____

_____

_____

_____

What must change in your life so that you are living in faith, hope, and love? How will you live it out?

_____

_____

_____

_____

_____

_____

What specific goal have you set for your Financial growth and refinement for this week? What is your progress?

_____

_____

Write the memory verse for this week: *1 Corinthians 15:57.*

_____

_____

_____

Write out three things you are grateful for today.

_____

_____

_____

Write out a prayer to God responding to today's lesson.

_____

_____

_____

_____

_____

_____

Ask, "Lord, what do You want to say to me personally about faith, hope, and love?"

_____

_____

_____

_____

_____

_____

_____

Reflection: How did you experience God in a special way today or yesterday?

_____

_____

_____

_____

_____

Pray for: Someone to be saved _____ someone to disciple _____

Date	Prayer Requests Received Today	How and when answered? (Come back and follow up as needed)

Notes

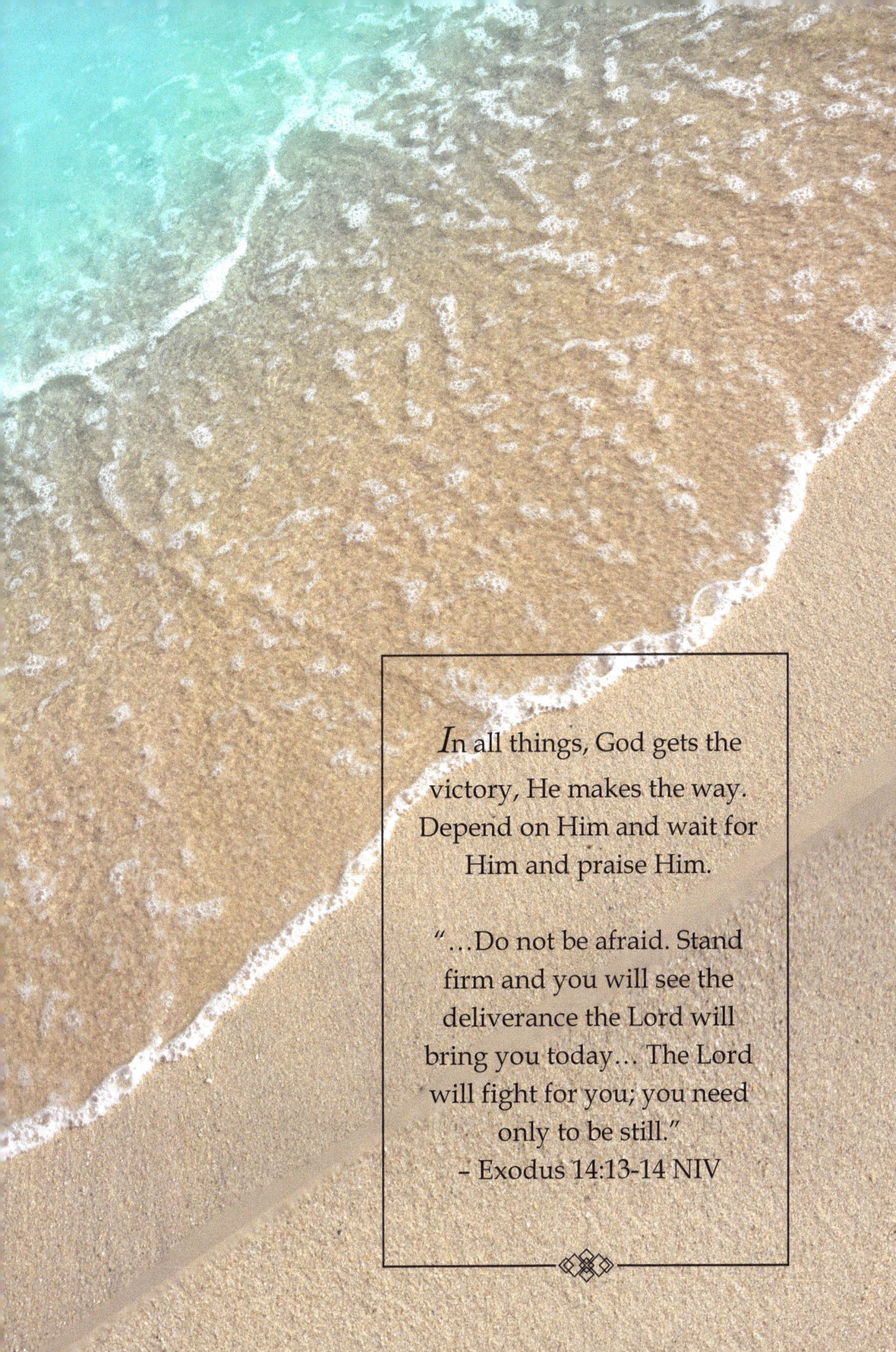

*I*n all things, God gets the victory, He makes the way. Depend on Him and wait for Him and praise Him.

"…Do not be afraid. Stand firm and you will see the deliverance the Lord will bring you today… The Lord will fight for you; you need only to be still."
– Exodus 14:13-14 NIV

Church Sermon Notes

Theme:

_____

_____

_____

Scriptures:

_____

_____

_____

Lessons:

_____

_____

_____

_____

_____

Application:

_____

_____

_____

_____

_____

Notes:

_____

_____

_____

_____

_____

Things to Remember from Week Twelve

Scriptures:

_____

_____

_____

Application:

_____

_____

_____

Goals Set:

_____

_____

_____

Memory Verse:

_____

_____

_____

Time with God:

_____

_____

_____

Reflection:

_____

_____

_____

Answered Prayers:

_____

_____

_____

Final Self-Evaluation

My life as of _____, 20_____

Spiritual	Yes	No	How Often
Do I read God's Word each day?			
Do I pray for my family, others, and myself?			
Am I attending a Bible-based Church?			
Do I testify about God to others?			
Mental			
Do I have a cheerful outlook?			
Do I listen to, watch, and read things that are uplifting and encouraging?			
Do I speak and react to others in a kind manner?			
Social/Emotional			
Do I honor and respect my spouse and family?			
Am I learning from a mentor or coach?			
Am I involved in a small group/community?			
Physical			
Do I eat/drink the right things each day?			
Do I exercise every day?			
Do I get enough rest daily?			
Financial			
Do I give to the Lord?			
Am I in debt?			
Do I save for an emergency fund?			
Total of columns			

Write what you are currently involved in doing. (Ex. Going to school, working at…, volunteering for…, names of close friends…, outdoor and indoor activities.)

_____

_____

_____

_____

_____

_____

_____

_____

_____

_____

_____

_____

_____

_____

_____

_____

_____

_____

_____

_____

_____

_____

_____

_____

_____

_____

_____

_____

Final Reflection

Take some time to reflect on key things that you learned that God revealed to you, or that you want to carry with you from this study.

_____

_____

_____

_____

_____

_____

Was there anything that seemed to be a repeating focus during each of the twelve weeks?

_____

_____

_____

_____

_____

In what ways have you grown in your relationship with God and recognizing His voice?

_____

_____

_____

_____

_____

Once you've taken time to reflect on your journey, consider the questions in the Appendices to continue your journey and growth.

Appendix A
Accountability Questions for Women

Accountability works ONLY IF you are accountable.
http://www.characterthatcounts.org

1. When do you spend regular time in prayer?

2. Have your thoughts been pure? Have you resisted lustful, envious thoughts or exposed yourself to explicit materials?

3. How do you feel about how you have managed personal, family, and/or business finances?

4. What three relationships have you nurtured most?

5. What has made it difficult to do your 100% best in the different roles in your life?

6. Have your words built up or tore down others or self?
   Have you exposed yourself or contributed to gossip?
   Have you been committed to your words?
   Have you put yourself in a better light to those around you?

7. Do you feel you missed any opportunities to talk to people about the Lord?

8. Have you taken care of your body through daily physical exercise and proper eating/sleeping habits?

9. Which fruit of the Spirit (See Galatians 5:22-23) have you had the hardest time living out and why?

10. Have you left anything hidden in answering these questions?

Appendix B
Accountability Questions for Men

Accountability works ONLY IF you are accountable.
http://www.characterthatcounts.org

1. Have you spent daily time in the Scriptures and in prayer?

2. Have you had any flirtatious or lustful attitudes, tempting thoughts, or exposed yourself to any explicit materials, which would not glorify God?

3. Have you been completely above reproach in your financial dealings?

4. Have you spent quality relationship time with family and friends?

5. Have you done your 100% best in your job and/or school?

6. Have you told any half-truths or outright lies, putting yourself in a better light to those around you?

7. Have you shared the Gospel with an unbeliever this Session?

8. Have you taken care of your body through daily physical exercise and proper eating/sleeping habits?

9. Have you allowed any person or circumstance to rob you of joy?

10. Have you lied to us on any of your answers today?

Appendix C
Scripture Index

Week 7: "For those who are led by the Spirit of God, are the children of God" (Romans 8:14).

Week 8: "Trust in the Lord with all your heart and lean not on your own understanding; in all your ways submit to Him, and He will make your paths straight" (Proverbs 3:5-6).

Week 9: "Until now you have not asked for anything in My name. Ask and you will receive, and your joy will be complete" (John 16:24).

Week 10: "This is the confidence we have in approaching God: that if we ask anything according to His will, He hears us. And if we know He hears us—whatever we ask—we know that we have what we asked of Him" (I John 5:14-15).

Week 11: "Do not conform to the pattern of this world but be transformed by the renewing of your mind. Then you will be able to evaluate and approve what God's will is –His good, pleasing, and perfect will" (Romans 12:2).

Week 12: "But thanks be to God! He gives us the victory through our Lord Jesus Christ (1 Corinthians 15:57).

Notes

SCHOOL OF THE SPIRIT

Three Powerful Benefits YOU Will Experience

1

You will learn to easily and daily hear God's voice

2

You will be able to live as Jesus did

3

You won't just study about God – you will have your own personal encounters with God

Take Your Place in God's Advancing Kingdom!

How far could you go with a Bible School in your pocket?

Go to: bwicministries.com/discipleship

Thank You!

Thank you so much for doing this Bible Study. I sincerely hope it has blessed you and impacted your life, your faith, and your intimacy with God. If so, give Him the glory, and would you help get it into more people's hands?

I would be so grateful if you shared with someone, and if you shared your honest review on the book page.

www.ingramcontent.com/pod-product-compliance
Lightning Source LLC
Chambersburg PA
CBHW041145120626
46547CB00020B/3112